GREAT BIBLE STORIES

REBECCA AT THE WELL

Adapted by Maxine Nodel　　**Illustrated by Norman Nodel**

BARONET BOOKS is a registered trademark of Playmore Inc., Publishers
and Waldman Publishing Corp., New York, N.Y.

BARONET BOOKS, NEW YORK, NEW YORK
Printed in China

When Abraham had already grown old, his son, Isaac, had turned into a fine young man.

One day Abraham spoke to his eldest servant, “Swear by the Lord, that you will go back to my country and find a wife for Isaac.”

So the servant took ten of his master's camels and traveled to the city of Nahor, in Mesopotamia.

Just outside the city, he made the camels kneel down before a well.

As night came on, the women of the city came out to the well to draw water.

Then the servant prayed, "O Lord God of my master, Abraham, hear my plan and send me good fortune."

The servant decided to say to one of the women drawing water, "Let down your pitcher, so that I may drink."

"If she is the wife, O Lord, you will have chosen for Isaac, let her say, 'Drink, and I will give your camel a drink also.'"

Before the servant had finished praying, a beautiful young woman went over to the well with her pitcher on her shoulder.

The servant approached her and said, “Let me, please, drink water from your pitcher.”

And the woman lowered her pitcher and said, "Drink, sir, and I will draw water for your camels."

The servant lifted his eyes with hope and promise. He felt that the Lord had answered his prayer.

"Whose daughter are you, and is there room in your father's house to spend the night?" asked the servant.

"I am Rebecca, grand-daughter of Nahor. We have straw and food for your camels and a room and food for you."

The servant looked up at God. “Blessed be the God of Abraham, for he has led me to the house of my master’s brother, Nahor.”

Then the servant removed a golden earring and two golden bracelets from his pocket.

The servant gave them to Rebecca and she ran home to tell everyone what had happened.

When Rebecca's brother, Laban, saw the jewelry, he ran out to Abraham's servant and said, "Come in, you whom the Lord has blessed."

Dinner was set before the servant, but he said, “Before I eat, I will tell you why I’m here.”

"I am the servant of Abraham, and I was sent to find a wife for his son, Isaac."

Rebecca's father replied, "Since this has been planned by the Lord, take Rebecca and let her be Isaac's wife."

But Rebecca's brother and mother insisted, "Let Rebecca stay with us ten days more and then she shall go with you."

"You should not hinder me," said the servant. "God has made my errand a success; I must return home to my master, Abraham."

"We will call Rebecca and ask her," said the family, and when Rebecca appeared, they asked,

"Will you go with this man?"

"I will go," she replied. So Rebecca and her maidens followed the servant and traveled to Abraham.

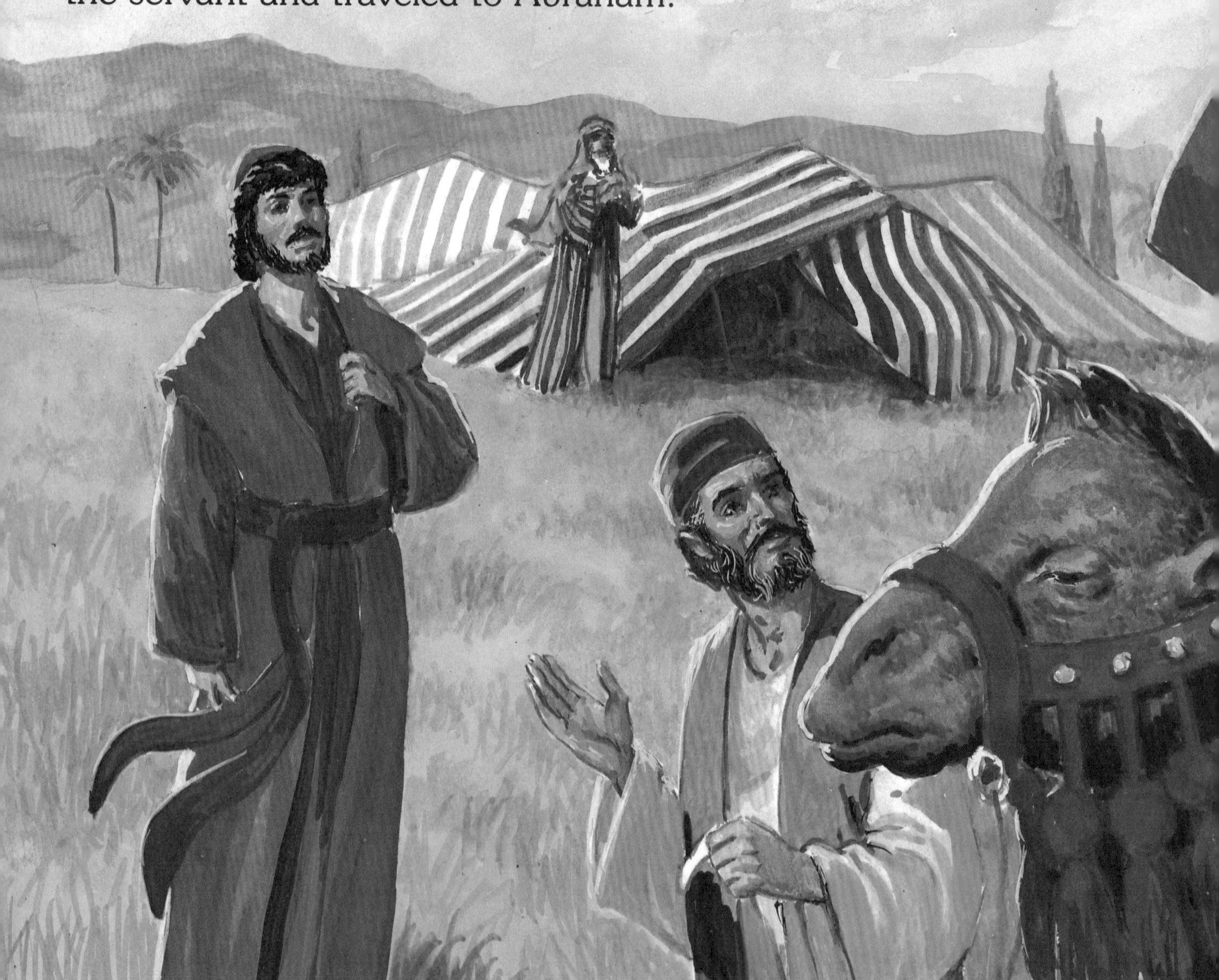

Rebecca married Isaac and they lived happily together.

When time passed, God blessed them with twin sons, Jacob and Esau.